THE
CROSS STITCH
TREASURY

THE
CROSS STITCH
TREASURY

CATS, DOGS & BIRDS

GREENWICH EDITIONS

This edition published in 1995 by
Greenwich Editions
Unit 7
202-8 New North Road
London N1 7BJ

Produced by Marshall Cavendish Books, London

ISBN 0 862 880 70X

British Library Cataloguing in Publication Data:
A catalogue record for this book is available from the British Library

Printed and bound in France by Partenaires

Some of this material has previously appeared in the Marshall Cavendish partwork *Discovering Needlecraft.*

Contents

Foreword

Cross-stitch is probably the most popular embroidery technique practised in today's busy world, and it is certainly one of the oldest forms of textile decoration. It is a simple stitch that can be learned and enjoyed by young children and skilled stitchers alike to create amazingly intricate and interesting pieces which can become works of art or family heirlooms.

In fact, cross-stitch is a passion, practised by young and old, hobbyists and professionals, laid-back and perfectionist, and those lucky enough to be addicted will find much in this collection of projects to tempt them. The designs range from small-scale items such as greetings cards to intricate pieces that are highly realistic interpretations of familiar objects. So, if you love cross-stitch, pick up your needle, choose your chart and begin ...

Counted cross-stitch

Probably the oldest embroidery stitch of all, and certainly one of the quickest and easiest, counted cross-stitch is worked all over the world, in countries as far removed from each other as Mexico and India.

Cross-stitch has many uses. It can be worked as an outline or border, or as a filling stitch, and lends itself particularly well to lettering and motifs. Worked on canvas, it is very hardwearing and so makes a good choice for upholstery.

Counted cross-stitch is usually stitched on special evenweave fabrics, such as aida, hardanger, linda or binca, or on canvas, because this makes it easier to count threads and the whole effect of the stitch depends on its regularity. Each cross-stitch should make a perfect square, being worked down and across over an equal number of threads.

Designs for counted cross-stitch are always presented in chart form, where one cross or symbol or block of colour denotes a single stitch. Using one of these charts is easy – you literally count your way across the design.

There are several ways of working basic cross-stitch. Choose your method according to the fabric or canvas you will be working on. When working cross-stitch on canvas, or only making the odd cross-stitch here and there, it is best to complete each cross before moving on to the next one.

If you are working cross-stitch in rows on evenweave material, first work a line of diagonals in one direction, then cover them with 'top' diagonals, working in the opposite direction. By doing this you get a more even tension and finish. A variation of this, called alternate cross-stitch involves working every other diagonal from right to left, then filling in the gaps by working another row of diagonals in the same direction, before working the top diagonals in the same way. This ensures an even more regular tension and so is a particularly good choice if you want to fill a very large area with cross-stitch.

One rule applies to all methods: the top diagonal stitches must always lie in the same direction. If they do not, they will reflect the light differently from the other stitches and will stand out clearly as mistakes. The only exception is when you actually want to produce an uneven or irregular effect.

OUTLINE STITCH

Use Holbein stitch, also known as double running stitch, in combination with cross-stitch to outline and emphasize solidly-stitched shapes and also to work decorative linear details. Like cross-stitch, Holbein stitch worked as an outline is most successful when sewn on an evenweave fabric so the fabric threads can be counted to ensure perfect regularity.

Holbein stitch looks exactly the same on both sides of the fabric. It can be worked in straight lines or stepped to make a zigzag line when outlining a diagonal row of cross-stitches. The finished result looks rather like a row of backstitch, at least on the front. All the stitches should be of identical length.

Cross-stitch motifs can be as varied and colourful as you wish. From floral designs and alphabets to geometric borders, plain or fancy, you can create some lovely effects. Don't stick to printed charts either – have a go at designing your very own motifs and borders. Take your inspirations from some of the stitched examples that appear here.

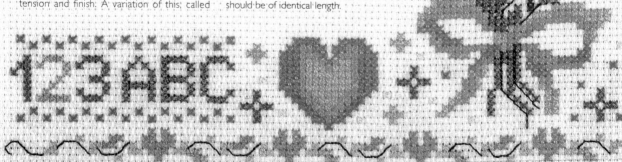

HOW TO WORK A SINGLE CROSS-STITCH

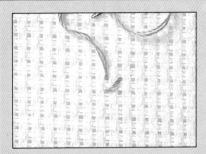 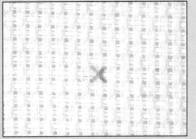

1 Make a diagonal stitch to the lower left, take the needle through to the back of the fabric and bring the needle back up at what will be the top left-hand corner of the cross.

2 Finish by taking the thread across the existing diagonal and inserting needle in bottom right-hand corner of cross. Count fabric threads to ensure each cross is worked over a square.

Various evenweave cottons and linens are specially produced with counted cross-stitch in mind. The most well-known is an evenweave cotton fabric called aida. Three of the samples below are made of the aida; the 22-count fabric is cotton hardanger. Each sample has a different 'count', which has been worked on the front in cross-stitch. The count refers to the number of holes in the fabric (those large enough to pass a needle and thread through) per inch. The holes are all exactly the same number of threads apart. As shown below, the count of your background fabric affects the size of each cross-stitch, and thus the scale and size of your finished design, quite considerably.

HOW TO WORK CROSS-STITCH IN ROWS

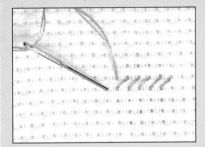 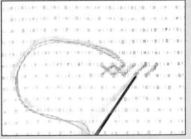

1 Make a diagonal stitch from top right to lower left. Bring needle out through the hole next to the start of the first stitch, ready to form the next, and continue.

2 At the end of the row change direction and complete the crosses by working another row of diagonals, this time from left to right, working each diagonal from upper left to lower right.

HOW TO WORK HOLBEIN STITCH AS AN OUTLINE

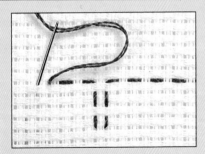 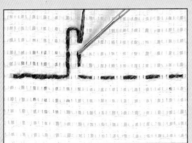 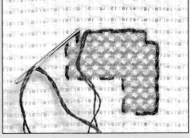

1 Work running stitches from right to left, following the outline of your shape. Each stitch should cover the same number of threads and the spaces in between should be the same size.

2 At the end of the row, turn work round and work back over the row just done, filling in the spaces with another row of running stitch. Keep the tension even at all times.

3 Outline a diagonal row of cross-stitch by alternately working horizontal and vertical running stitches. The Holbein stitch should outline the shape with a narrow, continuous line.

Good luck card

This little card will cover a wide variety of special occasions
and is quick and easy to work in cross-stitch.

Good luck card

YOU WILL NEED

- 8.5CM X 10CM WHITE 14-COUNT AIDA FABRIC
- MADEIRA 6-STRANDED EMBROIDERY COTTON, ONE SKEIN IN EACH OF THE FOLLOWING COLOURS: GREY 1802, MAUVE 0805, GREEN 1305, BLACK
- TAPESTRY NEEDLE
- 11.5CM X 9CM CARD MOUNT & ENVELOPE
- FABRIC GLUE

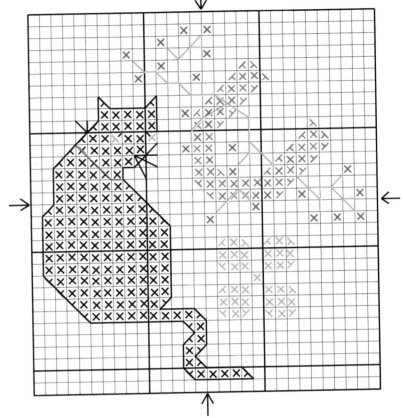

This good luck card is especially appropriate because it includes a collection of lucky symbols – a horse-shoe, a four-leaved clover, a black cat and a sprig of heather. Lucky symbols change their meanings as civilizations evolve and cultural beliefs alter. The black cat as a portent of good luck is a relatively modern notion in the West. The Chinese also credit cats with good fortune and the ability to banish evil spirits, but in Celtic times, cats symbolized evil and were used in ritual sacrifice.

ORDER OF WORK

Fold your piece of fabric in half both ways to find the centre and mark with a small cross using sewing thread. Follow the chart on this page to

work the good luck card design. Each symbol on the chart represents one stitch, and the colours used are appropriate to the thread colours.

Count outwards from the centre of the fabric and begin by stitching the cat, using two strands of black. Finish all the cross-stitches and the three-quarter stitches before working the backstitching. Next, work the horseshoe using two strands of grey, and the sprigs of heather using mauve. The foliage for both the clover and the heather is worked in green. Outline the cat and give it some whiskers, using one strand of black embroidery cotton.

MAKING UP THE CARD

Spread fabric glue sparingly over the central section of the card on the inside. Position the

A lucky black cat forms the main motif on the card. This is worked in black cross-stitch, with three-quarter stitches used to give a smooth outline. A purple collar completes the motif.

glued area of the card over the stitched design with the stitching central to the circular aper-ture. On the inside, carefully spread glue around the edges of the central section, avoid-ing the area where the fabric shows through the aperture. Fold the left-hand section of the card over to cover the fabric. Press down firmly to seal.

bright idea

If you wish to give your card a more elaborate feel, use felt pens, water-based paints or coloured pencils to add a border to the card mount. Trace a line around the circular aperture and go over it using a gold marker, or draw tiny clover leaves or horseshoes. Alternatively, embellish one of the bottom corners of the card with a sprig of heather.

Cute kittens

This pretty cross-stitch design features two tabby kittens with bows around their necks and is very reminiscent of Berlin woolwork pictures.

Cute kittens

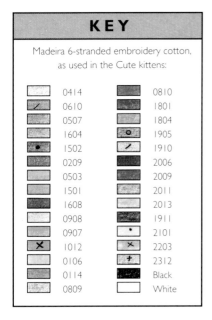

KEY

Madeira 6-stranded embroidery cotton,
as used in the Cute kittens:

☐ 0414		▤ 0810
◪ 0610		▨ 1801
▦ 0507		▨ 1804
▦ 1604		⊙ 1905
● 1502		◪ 1910
▦ 0209		▬ 2006
▦ 0503		▬ 2009
▨ 1501		▤ 2011
▦ 1608		▨ 2013
☐ 0908		▨ 1911
▨ 0907		• 2101
✕ 1012		✕ 2203
☐ 0106		✛ 2312
▨ 0114		■ Black
▨ 0809		☐ White

These two little tabby kittens, sitting on a checked cushion, are so realistic that you will want to pick them up and take them home. They both have pastel-coloured bows around their necks and a red geranium fills one corner of the picture.

The kittens' intricate shading is created by using Madeira 6-stranded embroidery cotton in a wide range of browns and golds with high-lights in white and grey. A tortoiseshell-effect frame and a cream mount complete the design, but these can be changed to suit any room setting of your choice.

BEFORE YOU START

Bind the edges of your aida fabric with either masking tape or bias binding, to prevent them from fraying as you stitch. If you use masking tape, ensure that you use one that is wide enough to cover the edges securely and that it is well stuck down onto the fabric. Fold the aida fabric lightly into four and mark the centre horizontal and vertical lines with running stitch. Use a bright-coloured sewing thread for these lines which can be worked over and then removed when the design is complete. Mark the corresponding centre point on the colour chart opposite using a pencil.

Mount the fabric in an embroidery hoop or slate frame if you wish. This will keep the fabric taut as you work and ensure that all your stitching is of an even tension. If you do use a hoop, great care must be taken when moving it around the fabric so that none of the previously worked stitching becomes damaged. A sheet of acid-free tissue paper placed between the aida fabric and the hoop may help

This little kitten, with its pretty pink bow, is worked on the left-hand side of the picture. It has blue eyes and a soft pink nose. The dark browns and gold that are used for the kitten's head are contrasted by its white chest stripes.

to prevent this – it will also help to keep the fabric clean around the edges of the hoop.

As there are a number of different shades of brown used to work the kitten design, fasten 45cm lengths of each colour on to a thread card and label them clearly with their skein numbers; this will help you to identify them more easily when you reach them on the chart.

STITCHING THE DESIGN

Each coloured square on the chart equals one cross-stitch which is worked using just two strands of the Madeira 6-stranded embroidery cotton in the needle. Follow the key on the left for the colours to use. Always finish one area of stitching before moving on to the next and avoid passing long strands of cotton across the back of the work as this may become caught up in subsequent stitching and cause the back of the work to become bulky. If this happens the picture my be difficult to mount and frame.

YOU WILL NEED

- 40CM X 35CM CREAM 14-COUNT AIDA FABRIC
- MADEIRA 6-STRANDED EMBROIDERY COTTON, ONE SKEIN IN EACH OF THE FOLLOWING COLOURS: PALE PINK 0503, DEEP PINK 0507, ORANGE 0209, PALE BLUE 0908, MID BLUE 0907, LIME GREEN 1501, BRIGHT GREEN 1502, OLIVE GREEN 1608, YELLOW 0106, YELLOW GOLD 0114, SKY BLUE 1012, SUGAR PINK 0414, DUSTY ROSE 0809, DARK ROSE 0810, DARK GREEN 1404, DARK GREY 1801, PALE GREY 1804, TAUPE 1905, BEIGE 1910, DARK BROWN 2006, GOLD BROWN 2011, MID BEIGE 2013, TAN BROWN 2009, MID TAUPE 1911, CREAM 2101, GREEN GOLD 2203, PINK BROWN 2312, MID PINK 0610, PALE GREEN 1604, BLACK, WHITE
- TAPESTRY NEEDLE

Never start your stitching with a knot, but leave a short end on the wrong side that can be worked over by the first few stitches. To finish the work off neatly, pass the needle back through a few stitches. At this point, work all the cross-stitching only, leaving the backstitch details until the design is complete.

Starting at the centre marked points on both the fabric and the chart, begin stitching the beige tabby kitten's paw. When this is complete, move on to stitch its face and body. Work the very small areas of colour, such as for the eyes and mouth, first and then fill in the larger areas around them. In this way you are less likely to make a mistake. When you have finished stitching the kitten, work its bow using three shades of blue.

For the brown-and-white kitten on the left, start by stitching the areas that adjoin those already worked for the beige kitten, stitching from the centre of the fabric towards the edges. Once again, end with the kitten's bow, which is worked in three shades of pink.

Once the two kittens are complete, stitch the checked cushion that surrounds them. This is worked in green with a slightly darker shade for the shadows and has a trellis pattern in dusty rose and deep pink. Finally, work the red geranium plant in the top right-hand corner. The flower petals are worked in red and pink

and have soft blue centres. Before you move on to work all the backstitching, check that you have not missed any cross-stitches as these will be difficult to add to the picture later.

BACKSTITCH DETAILS

Use two strands of the embroidery cotton in the needle for all the backstitching except the kittens' whiskers, which are worked with only one strand in the needle. Starting at the top right-hand corner of the picture, work the details on the geranium flower petals in deep pink (0507). This colour is also used to work the details on the pink bow. The leaf veins should be worked in dark green (1404); note that this is the only time that this colour is used.

Next, use sky blue (1012) to work the backstitching on the blue bow. To outline the beige kitten's paw and ear, use dark brown (2006). The kittens' mouths are worked using the dark grey (1801).

When you come to work the kittens whiskers, use only one strand of the dark brown embroidery cotton in the needle and work them in free backstitch. To work this, follow the lines marked on the chart but do not necessarily follow the holes of the aida fabric as you would do normally. Working through the centre of some stitches as well will help you to achieve a softer, curved line of

It is inevitable that occasionally you will make mistakes when stitching a complex design such as this. If you do need to unpick an area of stitching, prevent any of the surrounding stitches from becoming damaged by using a blunt-ended needle to carefully lift each leg of the stitch. You will probably be unable to re-use the unpicked cotton, so be careful that you do not run out of thread if you have to unpick large areas of the design.

stitching. Take care, though, that you still keep the stitches short and neat in the same way as you would do if you were following the holes in the aida fabric.

FINISHING TOUCHES

Remove the embroidery from the hoop, if one was used, and press the design carefully from the wrong side over a lightly padded surface. This will prevent the stitches from becoming flattened. Mount and frame the picture as required. If you use a mount board, check that it is acid-free or it may cause a discolouration of the fabric over a period of time.

STITCH DETAILS

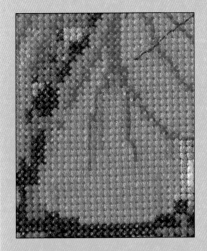

Three shades of pink are used to work the brown-and-white kitten's bow, which is also backstitched in deep pink. This is a perfect contrast to the dark fur.

The brown-and-white kitten has bright blue eyes with black and white pupils. Just below these is worked a small pink nose and a smiling grey mouth.

For the beige tabby kitten, a range of lighter browns and taupes has been used for the fur. This is highlighted with splashes of mid grey cotton.

Scotty dog scarf

Stitch these delightful dogs to immortalize a faithful friend.

These little dog motifs could be used to decorate a wide variety of garments, and children will find them especially charming. Work them singly on a shirt pocket or to decorate the front of a small pair of slippers. Stitch them using the chart on the following page.

Cut the wool fabric in half lengthwise to give two pieces 150cm x 30cm. Cut a piece of waste canvas 30cm x 10cm and tack it in position along the end of one of the pieces of fabric. Take care that it is positioned centrally and along the straight grain. Stretch the fabric in an embroidery hoop and mark the centre of the waste canvas.

Using cross-stitch and two strands of cotton, begin stitching the dogs at the centre point, working the cross-stitches firmly over the double threads of the canvas. When the dogs have been stitched, work the collars, using red for the black dogs and green for the white dogs. Remove the tacking threads, but do not remove the fabric from the hoop. Unravel the bottom of the waste canvas up to the first row of stitching. First pull out the vertical threads of the canvas and then the horizontal threads from under the design, dampening slightly if necessary. Remove the hoop and work the other end of the scarf to match.

MAKING UP THE SCARF

Press the design from the wrong side over a padded surface to prevent the stitches from becoming flattened. Place the two pieces of fabric together right sides facing and backstitch, or machine stitch, around the edges, leaving a small opening in one long side. Clip the corners and turn to the right side. Slip stitch the opening to close.

YOU WILL NEED

- 60CM OF 150CM WIDE DARK RED WOOL FABRIC
- MADEIRA 6-STRANDED EMBROIDERY COTTON: ONE SKEIN IN EACH OF BLACK, WHITE, RED 0510, GREEN 1305
- 60CM x 10CM 14-GAUGE WASTE CANVAS
- MATCHING SEWING THREAD
- TAPESTRY NEEDLE
- EMBROIDERY HOOP

Scotty dog scarf

Use the chart and key on this page to work the cross-stitch design for the Scotty dog motif. Each square on the chart represents one cross-stitch worked over one square of evenweave fabric. Before you start, follow the direction of the arrows to find the centre square so that you can position the design squarely on the fabric. Take care when matching each section of the design either side of the vertical 'centre' line.

KEY

Madeira cotton, as used in the Scotty dog scarf:

↑	Black
/	White
^	Green (1305)
o	Red (0510)
/	Backstitching using the collar colour

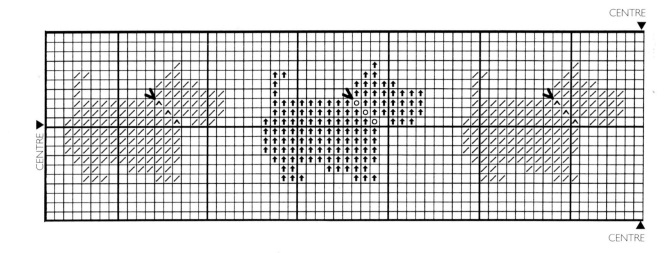

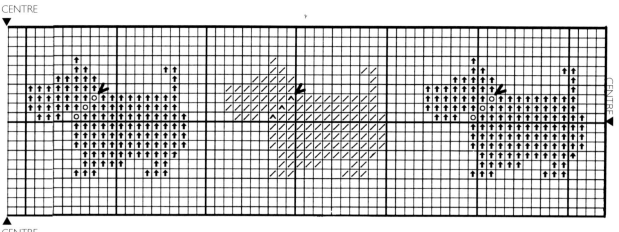

Mountain dog

The realistic effect which you can achieve with cross-stitch is very evident in this portrait of a Bernese mountain dog.

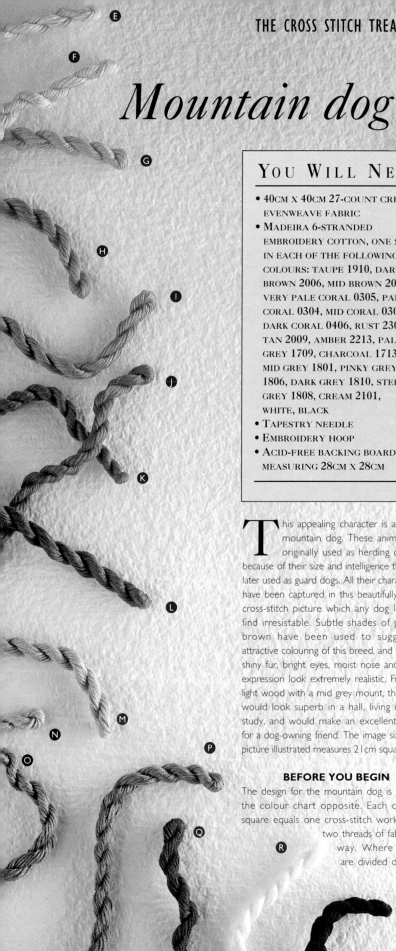

Mountain dog

YOU WILL NEED

- 40CM X 40CM 27-COUNT CREAM EVENWEAVE FABRIC
- MADEIRA 6-STRANDED EMBROIDERY COTTON, ONE SKEIN IN EACH OF THE FOLLOWING COLOURS: TAUPE 1910, DARK BROWN 2006, MID BROWN 2008, VERY PALE CORAL 0305, PALE CORAL 0304, MID CORAL 0303, DARK CORAL 0406, RUST 2306, TAN 2009, AMBER 2213, PALE GREY 1709, CHARCOAL 1713, MID GREY 1801, PINKY GREY 1806, DARK GREY 1810, STEEL GREY 1808, CREAM 2101, WHITE, BLACK
- TAPESTRY NEEDLE
- EMBROIDERY HOOP
- ACID-FREE BACKING BOARD MEASURING 28CM X 28CM

This appealing character is a Bernese mountain dog. These animals were originally used as herding dogs, but because of their size and intelligence they were later used as guard dogs. All their characteristics have been captured in this beautifully worked cross-stitch picture which any dog lover will find irresistable. Subtle shades of grey and brown have been used to suggest the attractive colouring of this breed, and the dog's shiny fur, bright eyes, moist nose and friendly expression look extremely realistic. Framed in light wood with a mid grey mount, the picture would look superb in a hall, living room or study, and would make an excellent present for a dog-owning friend. The image size of the picture illustrated measures 21cm square.

BEFORE YOU BEGIN

The design for the mountain dog is given on the colour chart opposite. Each coloured square equals one cross-stitch worked over two threads of fabric each way. Where squares are divided diagonally with half in one colour and half in another, work three-quarter and quarter cross-stitches (see the handy hint overleaf for how to work these part stitches). The key shows you which threads to use for each part of the design.

So that the evenweave fabric does not fray while you are working on it, oversew the edges or bind them with masking tape. Fold the fabric in half each way and mark the horizontal and vertical centres with lines of running stitches using a brightly coloured sewing thread. The centre of the chart is marked with arrows. This will help you to position the stitches correctly as you work the picture. As there are quite a few toning shades in the design, you may find it useful to sort your threads onto a project card. These are available from haberdashers and needlework shops, but it is simple to make your own. Punch a series of holes along the edge of strips of stiff card and loop your threads through; mark the thread number beside each one. It will then be easy to find each colour.

STITCHING THE DOG

Stretch the fabric in an embroidery hoop. This will help you to work with an even tension and will give a more professional-looking finish. Choose a hoop at least 25cm in diameter as this will be large enough to show the whole design at once and will save you having to move it around as you work. Remember, though, to remove the hoop at the end of each stitching session, as otherwise it can mark your fabric permanently.

With two strands of cotton in your needle, begin stitching centrally at the dog's mouth. To secure your thread end, leave a short length at the back of the fabric and work the first few

The twisted skeins on this page show the colours of Madeira 6-stranded embroidery cotton that were used to stitch the mountain dog picture. A wide range of shades is used within each colour to create realistic shading on the dog's fur and facial features.

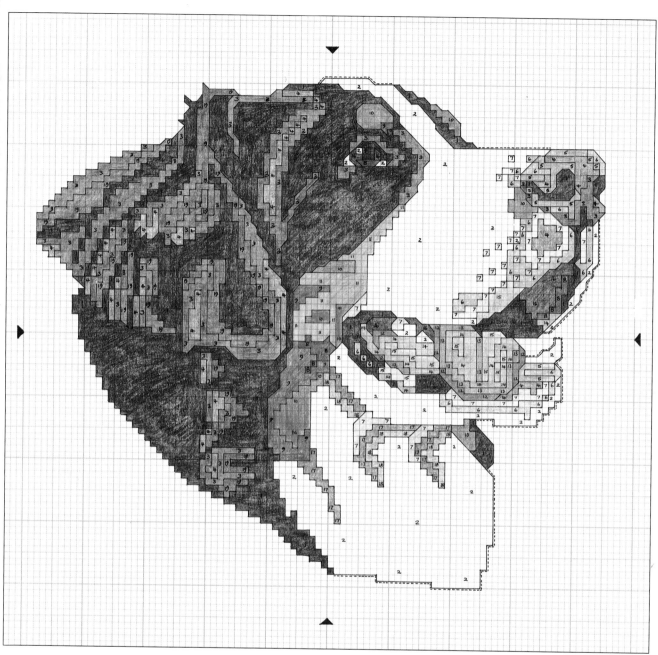

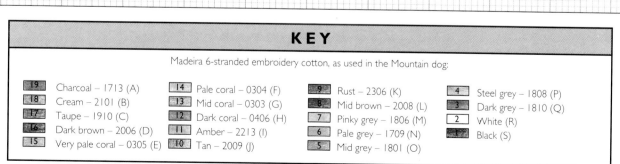

KEY

Madeira 6-stranded embroidery cotton, as used in the Mountain dog:

19 Charcoal – 1713 (A)	14 Pale coral – 0304 (F)	9 Rust – 2306 (K)	4 Steel grey – 1808 (P)
18 Cream – 2101 (B)	13 Mid coral – 0303 (G)	8 Mid brown – 2008 (L)	3 Dark grey – 1810 (Q)
17 Taupe – 1910 (C)	12 Dark coral – 0406 (H)	7 Pinky grey – 1806 (M)	2 White (R)
16 Dark brown – 2006 (D)	11 Amber – 2213 (I)	6 Pale grey – 1709 (N)	1 Black (S)
15 Very pale coral – 0305 (E)	10 Tan – 2009 (J)	5 Mid grey – 1801 (O)	

STITCH DETAILS

The dog's ears are worked in charcoal, steel grey, dark grey and black to give the fur depth and shading.

For the dog's nose, use the paler shades of grey which gradually fade to white and become the fur on his muzzle.

The dog's tongue is worked using the four shades of coral. The roof of his mouth is worked in dark brown and mid brown.

stitches over it. To finish off neatly, pass the needle through the last few stitches at the back and cut the thread off short so that it does not get caught up in subsequent stitching. The dog's mouth is worked in shades of grey and black with dark brown (2006) and mid brown (2008) in some places. The pink tongue is stitched in four shades of coral, ranging from very pale (0305) to dark (0406). Finish one area of colour at a time and remember not to carry long strands of thread across the back of the fabric, as these may show through at the front, especially when working with dark colours. They may also cause a lumpy effect when the picture is mounted.

Next stitch the brown area of the dog's face, using mid brown, tan (2009), rust (2306) and amber (2213). The creases at his jawline are worked in paler shades of taupe (1910), pinky grey (1806) and cream (2101). You can now work the large area of white which forms the dog's muzzle and chest. His fur is shaded using steel grey (1808), pinky grey and pale grey (1709) around his nose, which is worked in black with steel grey, pale grey and dark grey (1810).

Finally work the dark areas of the dog's face, using mainly black with shades of grey to show the creases. The dog's realistically shaped

ear is worked in the same shades of grey – dark grey, steel grey and charcoal (1713). Add the bright eye in black, white, dark brown and mid brown, and the highlights over the eyes in tan and rust.

When all the cross-stitching is complete, outline the white areas with backstitch, using one strand of pinky grey. This adds slight definition where the white cotton meets the cream background fabric. The backstitch areas are indicated by the dotted lines on the chart.

FINISHING OFF THE PICTURE

When all the embroidery is complete, check that you have not missed out any stitches as it will be difficult to rectify this once the picture is mounted over board and framed. Remove the brightly coloured running stitches which marked the centre lines, and trim off any thread ends which might show through to the right side of the fabric.

Press the work from the wrong side over a lightly padded surface so as not to flatten the stitches. Place face down on a table and lay the mounting board centrally on top. Turn the excess fabric to the back and secure with masking tape. Alternatively, you can lace the fabric with string pulled tight across the back of the mounting board. Frame your picture as you

wish. A neutral-coloured mount and frame will be most suitable for the natural colours used in the picture.

handy

To achieve a smooth diagonal line in a cross-stitch design such as this one of the mountain dog, you can work three-quarter and quarter cross-stitches in two colours rather than complete ones in a single colour. Examples of this technique are on the top of the dog's mouth, and also on his face where the black area meets the brown area.

Wherever you see a square on the chart divided diagonally, with half in one colour and half in another, work one of the colours as a quarter stitch going from one corner into the centre. Complete the stitch with a three-quarter stitch in the second colour; this has a short stitch from the opposite corner to the centre and a longer diagonal worked in the usual way. If the divided square is at the edge of the design, simply work a three-quarter cross-stitch in the colour shown. This will give you a smooth slanting line, such as the one on the tip of the dog's nose.

hint

Dalmatian picture

Enjoy stitching a portrait of one of the most distinctive of all the dog breeds – the Dalmatian.

Dalmatian picture

This soulful-looking Dalmatian is the second in our series of portraits of dogs worked in cross-stitch. Like the first picture – the Bernese mountain dog featured on pages 17-20 – this stitched Dalmatian is extremely lifelike and is sure to appeal to any dog-lover.

Born with just a few spots, the growing Dalmatian puppy gradually develops its distinctive pattern of spotted markings which increase in size and number as the dog grows older. These spots give the dog a very appealing and dapper appearance, making it a firm favourite with many pet owners. The dog in our picture has an attractive covering of spots, as well as beautiful deep brown eyes and an enquiring nose. Stitch him as a companion for the mountain dog or as a gift for a Dalmatian enthusiast.

PREPARING FOR STITCHING

The colour chart for the Dalmatian picture is given on the opposite page. The key which accompanies it shows you which colours of embroidery cotton to use for the stitching.

Each square on the chart equals one cross-stitch worked over two threads of fabric each way. Some of the squares on the chart are divided in half diagonally, with half in one colour and half in another. Where these come within the dog's head, such as on his nose and eyes, use three-quarter and quarter cross-stitches. Where the divided squares are around the edge of the head, work three-quarter stitches only (see the handy hint on page 20 for more information about how to work and

use these divided stitches). By using this technique, you will avoid the stepped effect that full cross-stitches give when used diagonally. The dog will have a much smoother outline and a more realistic appearance generally.

So that the evenweave fabric does not fray while you are working on it, oversew the raw edges or bind them with masking tape. Fold the fabric lightly in half each way and mark the centre lines with running stitches in a brightly-coloured sewing thread. These lines can be worked over and then removed when the

YOU WILL NEED

- 40CM X 40CM 27-COUNT CREAM EVENWEAVE FABRIC
- MADEIRA 6-STRANDED EMBROIDERY COTTON, ONE SKEIN IN EACH OF THE FOLLOWING COLOURS: CHESTNUT BROWN 2007, DARK BROWN 2006, CREAM 2101, FAWN 1910, PALE BROWN 1911, TAN 2311, PINKY BROWN 2312, PEACH 0304, FLESH 0305, MID GREY 1801, DARK GREY 1713; 2 SKEINS IN EACH OF WHITE, BLACK
- TAPESTRY NEEDLE
- EMBROIDERY HOOP
- ACID-FREE BACKING BOARD MEASURING ABOUT 28CM X 28CM

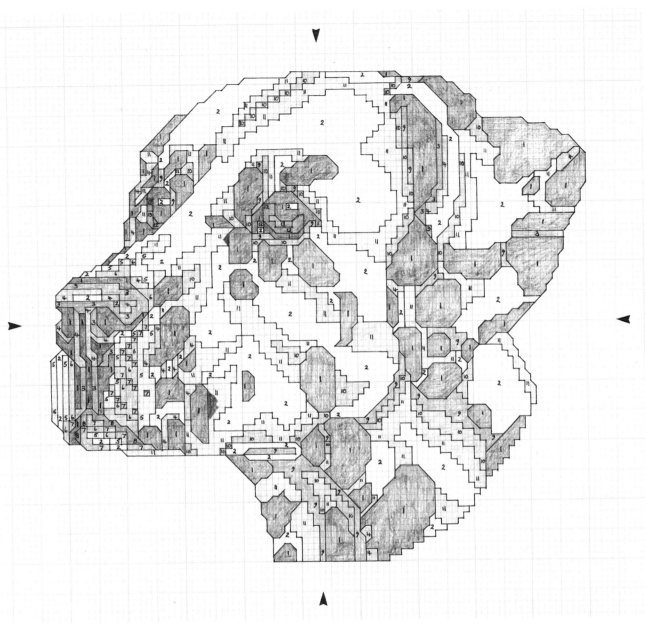

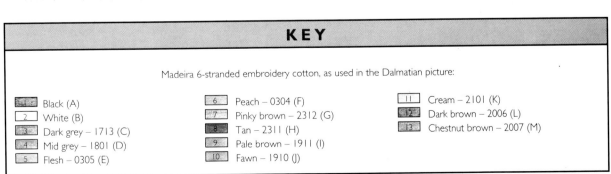

KEY

Madeira 6-stranded embroidery cotton, as used in the Dalmatian picture:

1 Black (A)	6 Peach – 0304 (F)	11 Cream – 2101 (K)
2 White (B)	7 Pinky brown – 2312 (G)	12 Dark brown – 2006 (L)
3 Dark grey – 1713 (C)	8 Tan – 2311 (H)	13 Chestnut brown – 2007 (M)
4 Mid grey – 1801 (D)	9 Pale brown – 1911 (I)	
5 Flesh – 0305 (E)	10 Fawn – 1910 (J)	

design is complete. Mark the centre of the chart in pencil to correspond. This will help you to position the stitches correctly as you work the picture.

As there are quite a few toning shades in the design, you might find it useful to sort your threads onto project cards. To make your own, simply punch a row of holes along the edge of two or three strips of stiff card and loop 45cm lengths of the embroidery cotton through them. Mark the thread colour and number beside each one. It will then be easy to find the correct shade as you need it.

STITCHING THE DOG

Stretch the fabric in an embroidery hoop to help you work with an even tension. Choose a hoop at least 25cm in diameter as this will be large enough to show the whole design at once, which will save you from having to move it around as you work. Remember, though, to remove the embroidery hoop at the end of each stitching session so that it does not mark your fabric permanently.

The cross-stitch embroidery is worked with two strands of cotton in the needle throughout. To secure your thread at the beginning, leave a short length at the back of the fabric and work the first few stitches over it. To finish off neatly, pass the needle under the last few stitches at the back and cut the thread end off short, so that it does not get caught up in subsequent stitching.

Begin stitching centrally by working the black marking in the middle of the dog's cheek. Then begin filling in the white and cream (2101) areas of the dog's face, adding more of the black spots as you come to them on the chart. Slightly deeper shading is worked in fawn (1910).

When you have worked the central part of the dog's face, stitch his soulful eye in black and dark brown (2006) with a tiny amount of chestnut brown (2007). The highlight is added in white. Then stitch his other eye in the same way. The Dalmatian's moist nose is worked in black and white with two shades of grey. All around his nose, his velvety muzzle is stitched in delicate tones of peach (0304) and flesh (0305) with tan (2311) and pinky brown (2312) shading. This is bordered by more black spots with mid grey (1801) areas.

On the right of the Dalmatian's head, work his ear in the same colours as the rest of his face, adding mid grey shading. Finish off the head by stitching the jawline and neck. The deepest shading, which outlines the jawline and extends down the neck, is pale brown (1911).

FINISHING OFF THE PICTURE

When you have completed all the embroidery, double-check to make sure that you have not left out any stitches by mistake, as it is difficult to rectify this once the picture is mounted. Using a blunt-ended needle, carefully remove the brightly-coloured running stitches which

handy

If you bind the inner ring of your embroidery hoop, you will find that it grips the fabric better and will be less likely to mark. Use opened-out bias binding or a strip of fine cotton fabric for this. Wind it around the ring, keeping it flat and overlapping it slightly as you go. Secure the end of the binding with a few stitches on the inside of the ring.

hint

marked the centre lines. Trim off any thread ends which might show through on the right side of the work, especially black ones that are more likely to look unsightly through the light-coloured linen fabric.

Press the embroidery from the wrong side over a padded surface so that you do not flatten the stitching. Place the picture face down on a table and lay the backing board on top. Turn the excess fabric to the back and secure it with masking tape, making sure the stitched area is in the centre. Alternatively, you can lace the fabric with string pulled tight across the back of the backing board. Then mount and frame your picture as you wish. As in the Mountain dog picture on pages 17–20, a plain wooden or neutral-coloured frame will probably be most suitable for the natural colours used in the picture.

STITCH DETAILS

The Dalmatian in this picture has beautiful eyes in a rich brown. The tiny white highlights give them a sparkle.

Work the smooth, velvety muzzle in delicate peach tones and the shiny nose in black with two shades of grey.

The subtle shadow areas on the dog's neck are achieved with bands of cream and very pale brown tones.

Emperor penguins

Anyone with an interest in wildlife will love this cross-stitch picture of an emperor penguin family.

Emperor penguins

The emperor penguin, which lives on the Antarctic icepack, is the largest of the seabirds and is extremely hardy as it has to survive in temperatures as low as -20°C. Penguin pairs are excellent parents, taking it in turns to incubate their single egg and then to catch food for their chick.

This appealing picture of an emperor penguin family shows a new-born chick huddling underneath its mother to keep warm, while its father bends his head to watch his offspring. The little group has been cleverly composed so that the penguins' bodies curve inwards towards the centre, making a very pleasing design. The colours are realistic as these penguins have bright orange stripes on their beaks and also have orange markings on their heads, fading out to creamy yellow. The body feathers of the chicks are grey before they develop their distinctive black-and-white plumage.

Worked almost entirely in cross-stitch with some backstitched outlines, this picture is not difficult to embroider and would suit beginners and more experienced stitchers alike. The picture area inside the mount measures 27cm by 30.5cm.

BEFORE YOU BEGIN

The chart for the penguin picture is shown on the opposite page. Each coloured square equals one cross-stitch worked over one square of the aida fabric. The white squares on the penguins' bodies show white cross-stitching, but the white background is left as unstitched fabric. Where squares are shown divided diagonally with half in one colour and half in another, work three-quarter and quarter cross-stitches (see the handy hint on page 20 for details of how to work these). The backstitch outlines around the eyes, chests and stomachs of the parent birds are shown by broken lines. The key indicates which colours of stranded cotton to use for each part of the chart.

Before you begin, oversew the edges of the aida fabric to prevent it from fraying. Fold the fabric in half each way and mark the centre creases with lines of running stitches in a brightly coloured sewing thread which can be removed when the embroidery is complete. Following the arrows, mark the centre lines on the chart in pencil to correspond. This will make it easier to follow the chart and place the stitches correctly.

As a wide range of greys has been used for the penguins' plumage in this picture, you may find it helpful to sort your stranded cotton onto project cards. These can be purchased from good needlecraft or haberdashery departments, but you can make your own by punching holes along strips of card and then looping the stranded cotton through them. Mark the colour name and number beside each one and you will then be able to locate them quickly as you need them.

STITCHING THE PENGUINS

If you wish, mount the fabric in a large embroidery hoop or work on a slate frame. This will keep the aida taut as you stitch, enabling you to achieve an even tension more easily. Using two strands of embroidery cotton in the needle for all the cross-stitching, begin

KEY

Madeira 6-stranded embroidery cotton, as used in the Emperor penguins:

1	Black	9	2006
2	White	10	2013
3	1713	11	1912
4	0208	12	1801
5	0207	13	1709
6	0202	14	1806
7	0114	15	1808
8	0111	16	1708

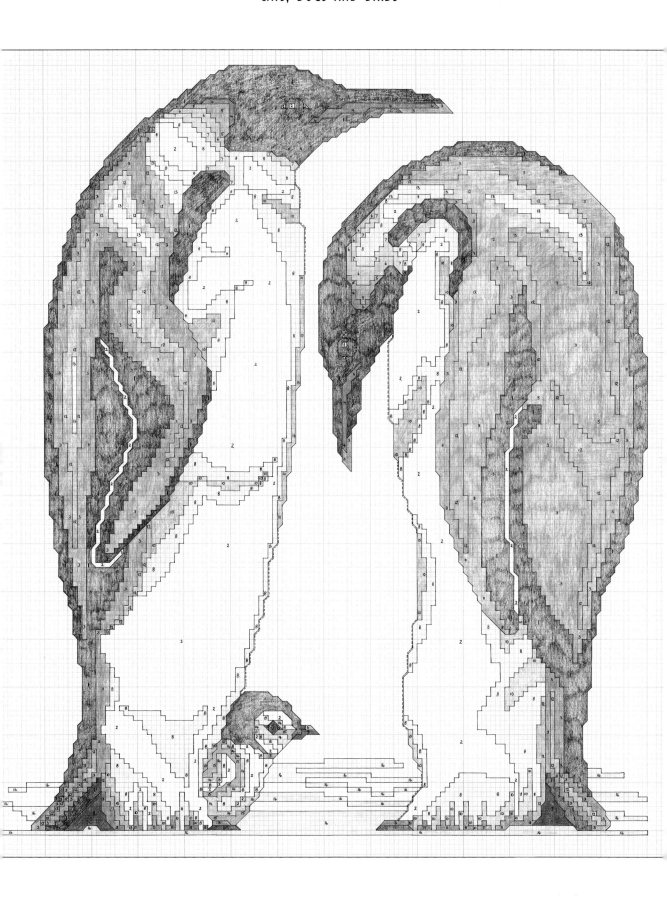

stitching centrally at the stooping penguin's beak. Use charcoal (1713) and black for the main part of the beak and burnt orange (0208) for the stripe. Progress up the head with the black cotton, adding the eye and the eye highlights with one complete cross-stitch and two three-quarter cross-stitches in white. Then stitch the colourful markings on the neck in shades of orange and yellow.

Continue stitching the stooping penguin by working his back and wings in various shades of grey, ranging from pale grey (1709) to charcoal. The edges of his wings and body are black. Complete the penguin by stitching his chest and stomach in white cotton with pale yellow (0111) and pale honey (2013) shading. There is a small amount of dark brown (2006) shading beneath his tail and some mink (1912) definition at the base of his body.

Now move across to the mother penguin on the left. She is worked in the same way as the male penguin, with similar colouring. The chick nestling at her feet is stitched in shades of grey with a black head and pale yellow markings. Its beak is tangerine (0202) and dark brown. To complete the cross-stitching, work the shading on the ice with horizontal rows of blue grey (1708).

When all the cross-stitching is complete, add the outlines in backstitch. Use two strands of steel grey (1801) cotton to surround the eyes of the parent birds with a circle, and one strand of pale honey (2013) cotton to outline the penguins' chests and stomachs. This will help to separate the white stitching from the white aida fabric.

FINISHING OFF

When the embroidery is complete, remove the brightly coloured running stitches and check to make sure you have not missed out any cross-stitches. Then press the work from the wrong side over a padded surface so as not to flatten the embroidery.

Cut a piece of stiff acid-free card to fit an existing frame or to the size you require. Stretch the embroidery over the card, securing it at the back with masking tape or by lacing it tightly with string pulled across the back. Mount and frame the picture as you wish. We have chosen a pale grey mount to echo the mainly monochrome colouring of the penguins and to emphasize the 'icy' feel of the picture, and have added a simple black frame to complement this.

STITCH DETAILS

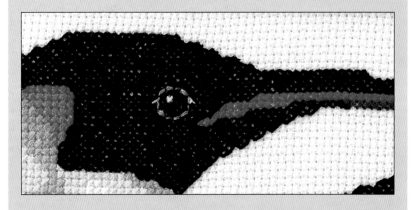

The parent penguins' eyes are emphasized with circles of steel grey backstitching, which is worked using two strands of embroidery cotton in the needle.

The penguin chick's plumage is slightly different from his parents' colouring to look soft and downy, but he still has the distinctive orange beak stripe.

Orange shading on the neck, fading to pale yellow and then to white on the chest, is a characteristic feature of the emperor penguin's plumage.

Valentine card

Combine traditional symbols of doves and hearts on this simple cross-stitch card to create the perfect Valentine gift.

Valentine card

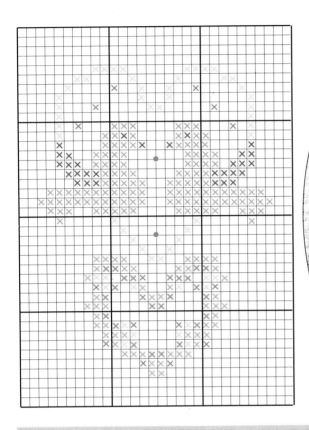

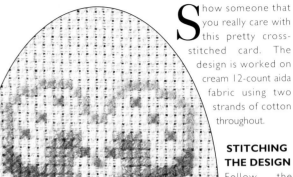

Show someone that you really care with this pretty cross-stitched card. The design is worked on cream 12-count aida fabric using two strands of cotton throughout.

STITCHING THE DESIGN
Follow the chart, with each square representing one stitch on the fabric, and work your way out from the central point. Find this by folding the aida in half and then in half again in the opposite direction. Start with the body of the birds in light blue, moving outwards to their wings in darker blue, and then work the large heart around them using pale pink. Stitch the smaller heart below using greens and pinks. Complete the design by working dark pink French knots as marked by a dot on the chart. For making up instructions, see page 10.

STITCHING THE DESIGN

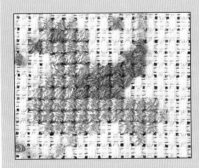

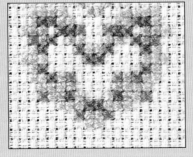

Stitch the bodies of the doves in light blue and then work their wings in a darker blue – you may find it easier to work the bodies first. The wings are given a curved outline underneath by working one three-quarter cross-stitch (see page 20) at the end of the second row, starting from the bottom of the wing.

To work the green and pink heart, stitch each colour separately, starting with the lighter pink. Make sure all the top diagonals of the crosses lie in the same direction to produce small, neat crosses. It is helpful to secure each thread end before moving onto the next colour so that the threads do not tangle.

YOU WILL NEED

- 10CM X 7.5CM CREAM 14-COUNT AIDA FABRIC
- MADEIRA 6-STRANDED EMBROIDERY COTTON, ONE SKEIN IN EACH OF THE FOLLOWING COLOURS: LIGHT BLUE 0901, BLUE 1012, LIGHT PINK 0503, PINK 0609, LIGHT GREEN 1209, GREEN 1203
- TAPESTRY NEEDLE
- 11.5CM X 9CM CARD MOUNT & ENVELOPE
- FABRIC GLUE

Wedding bookmark

With embroidered doves and ribbons this traditional cross-stitch bookmark
will make a perfect gift for a special day.

Wedding bookmark

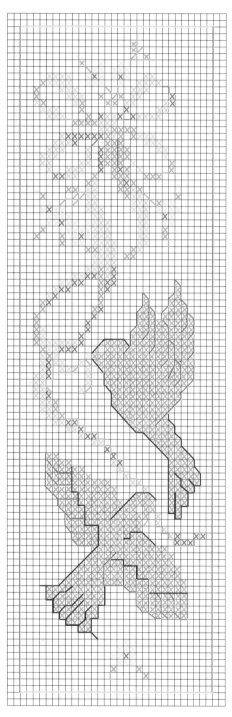

Awedding is probably the most important day in a couple's life and what better way to commemorate it than with this pretty cross-stitch bookmark worked on 14-count white aida fabric in shades of blue, pink, grey, yellow and green embroidery cotton?

STARTING TO STITCH

First find the centre of the fabric by folding it in half and then in half again. Tack the centre lines with coloured thread which can be worked over and removed when the design is complete. Following the chart on the left, work the design in cross-stitch using two strands of cotton throughout.

Once you have embroidered all the motifs in cross-stitch, outline as indicated on the chart using backstitch. Work round the birds' outer wings using dark pink and the bodies using dark grey. Outline the thinner areas of the ribbon using dark blue and dark pink. To complete, backstitch the frame using dark pink for the sides and pale pink for the top and bottom.

FINISHING TOUCHES

Using a pair of sharp embroidery scissors, cut around the bookmark to leave a three-square wide border.

Remove threads to within one aida square of the pink backstitch frame to create a fringed edging.

YOU WILL NEED

- **6.25CM X 20CM WHITE 14-COUNT AIDA FABRIC**
- **MADEIRA 6-STRANDED EMBROIDERY COTTON, ONE SKEIN IN EACH OF THE FOLLOWING COLOURS: DARK GREY 1801, GREY 1805, PALE PINK 0503, DARK PINK 0505, LIGHT BLUE 0908, DARK BLUE 0910, GREEN 1211, YELLOW 0110**
- **TAPESTRY NEEDLE**